How to Get Your Ex Back

Win Back Your Ex and Rebuild Your Relationship

Jane Wymer

This book is dedicated to anyone who has endured a broken heart from a relationship that could have been or should have been.

It is up to you to determine if that love is worth reclaiming. Always remember to love yourself first and others will follow.

Copyright Act of 1976, the scanning, uploading and electronic sharing of any part of this book without the explicit written consent or permission of the publisher constitutes unlawful piracy and the theft of intellectual property.

If you would like to use material or content from this book (other than for review purposes), prior written permission must be obtained from the publisher.

You can contact the publishing company at admin@speedypublishing.com. Thank you for not infringing on the author's rights.

Speedy Publishing LLC (c) 2014
40 E. Main St., #1156
Newark, DE 19711
www.speedypublishing.co

Ordering Information:
Quantity sales; Special discounts are available on quantity purchases by corporations, associations, and others. For details, contact the "Special Sales Department" at the address above.

This is a reprint book.

Manufactured in the United States of America

Table of Contents

Publisher's Notes i

Chapter 1: Introduction 1

Chapter 2: Perception After The Fact 3

Chapter 3: Take A Time Out And Focus On You 7

Chapter 4: Re-Evaluate Your Ex 10

Chapter 5: Get Rid Of Old Baggage 15

Chapter 6: Begging Never Works Out In The Long Run 18

Chapter 7: Avoid These 10 Mistakes When Trying To Win Back Your Ex 21

Chapter 8: Tips To Get Your Ex To Fall For You Again 26

Chapter 9: 10 Flirting Tips To Win Back Your Ex 30

Chapter 10: First move 36

Chapter 11: Getting Reacquainted With Each Other Again ... 39

Chapter 12: When Should You Have "The Talk" 43

Chapter 13: Cherish And Develop Your Relationship 47

Chapter 14: Knowing When To Move On 51

Chapter 15: Conclusion 54

Meet the Author 56

Publisher's Notes

Disclaimer

This publication is intended to provide helpful and informative material. It is not intended to diagnose, treat, cure, or prevent any health problem or condition, nor is intended to replace the advice of a physician. No action should be taken solely on the contents of this book. Always consult your physician or qualified health-care professional on any matters regarding your health and before adopting any suggestions in this book or drawing inferences from it.

The author and publisher specifically disclaim all responsibility for any liability, loss or risk, personal or otherwise, which is incurred as a consequence, directly or indirectly, from the use or application of any contents of this book.

Any and all product names referenced within this book are the trademarks of their respective owners. None of these owners have sponsored, authorized, endorsed, or approved this book.

Always read all information provided by the manufacturers' product labels before using their products. The author and publisher are not responsible for claims made by manufacturers.

Chapter 1: Introduction

You are reading this book for one reason: you lost someone that you love and you want to get them back. If it helps, you are not alone. Just about everyone who has lived long enough to fall in love has experienced what you are going through right now. Losing someone that you are in love with can be very painful and the sense of loss can overwhelm you. Your initial instinct will probably be to do whatever you can to get them back. But sometimes it is better to take a few steps back and evaluate the situation to avoid making the same mistakes again.

By the time, you are through reading this book, you will know:

- What caused the relationship to end
- If the relationship is really worth saving
- How to rekindle the romance
- Where to go after the "honeymoon" stage
- What to do if the relationship still won't work

Whether you are the person who ended the relationship or the one who got dumped; whether you were cheated on or did the cheating; whether you were married, dating or "just friends" this book will help you get the love of your life back. All of your sleepless nights are not over yet, but you will soon be able to see the light at the end of the lonely tunnel.

Be warned, though, a relationship will not be repaired overnight, and it will not be easy. Depending on the extent of the damage to the relationship it may take months or even years to get back to a truly healthy relationship. If you are willing to try and work hard at the relationship, though, you will be rewarded. Makeup sex has a reputation of being good for a reason...making it through hard times together only makes the good times sweeter.

So, get comfy and get ready to change your relationship. Be prepared to be brutally honest with yourself about what went wrong and what you can do to fix it. This book will not help you any if you are looking for someone to tell you that you are perfect and the other person needs to change for you. Relationships do not fail because of one person. No matter the circumstances, you must be willing to take at least some responsibility for what went wrong to start making it right.

Now...Let's get you ready to discover the joy of claiming back your ex.

Chapter 2: Perception After The Fact

Looking back on your failed relationship, you can probably pinpoint the moment when things ended. It was a phone call or a knockdown, drag-out fight in the living room or a text message that ended it all. But that isn't the reason the relationship ended. Even relationships that end because of the first instance of physical abuse almost always have underlying problems that led up to the demise of the relationship.

Figuring out what went wrong in the relationship is the first step in starting to fix things. This is one of the more difficult chapters in this book because it forces you to objectively look at the relationship that you are still emotionally hurting over. You may need to employ a friend or family member who knows you and your ex well to help you with this phase of the process. If you have a hard time figuring out what went wrong, ask for a second opinion.

Most relationships end for one of a handful of reasons: either one of you cheated, you were fighting about something (the divorce papers call this "irreconcilable differences"), one or both of you have emotional issues from your past that affected your relationship, the spark just seemed to die for one or both of you, or there were unhealthy circumstances like physical or emotional abuse. I'm sure there are other reasons that relationships end, but for the majority of us, it will fall under one of these categories.

As you read through the rest of this chapter, consider getting a notebook and pen. Make notes about your thoughts as you read. Try not to edit your thoughts too much before putting them down on paper. You may be surprised by what you discover.

Cheating

Unfortunately, cheating is a very common reason that relationships end. The hurt and betrayal are often too much for someone to take. Cheating is rarely ever the only problem in a relationship, though. You don't cheat on someone that you have a healthy, meaningful relationship with unless there are extenuating circumstances (like sexual abuse in your past).

More often than not, cheaters feel neglected or unwanted by the person they are with. They find someone who makes them feel the way that they felt when they first met their significant other and things spiral out of control from there. The problem with this euphoria is that it is how every relationship starts...before you really know each other well enough to see the good and the bad in the other person.

So, whether you did the cheating or were cheated on, look at the things that led up to the cheating. Work, kids, stress and lack of time together are some major things that drive the wedge in to begin with. It might not even be a bad thing that drove you apart to start. Maybe one of you worked too much trying to provide for both of you. Look for the cause of the cheating but try not to lay blame. Finding the cause will help you know what to work harder on in the future.

Fighting

This section alone could fill the entire book. Fighting is very broad for a reason. Everyone fights about something different. Maybe it was a pet peeve or difference of opinion. It doesn't matter what it is, what matters is that you are trying to get this person back.

Fighting is very passionate, and can lead to saying and doing things that you would never do otherwise. Think about whatever you were fighting about constantly. You may need to make a list to keep track. You shouldn't be surprised to see the list cover just a few themes though.

Now consider whether those things are worth losing the relationship over. They may be, but more likely, they are things that – with a calmer temper –you see as foolish. Learning to change the way that you fight and that you view another person while fighting will help you improve the relationship.

Past Issues

Relationships are a molding together of lives, and that includes pasts. We all have one, and we all have pain that we have overcome. If you have issues from childhood or past relationships that have affected your trust and ability to have a healthy relationship, identifying them is the first step to taking back control of your life.

To figure out what is holding you back (if it isn't obvious), try what writers call free writing. Just starting writing about yourself – not the failed relationship – concentrating on feelings and times in your life that defined who you are. Don't stop to think about what you're writing; just let the words and emotions flow onto the paper.

After you have found the problem, or if this exercise didn't reveal the issues, you may want to consider seeing a professional to help you work through those problems. Often our problems seem so shameful or so big that we don't want to share them, but if your lost love is worth getting back then you will do what you have to heal yourself.

Spark Died

There's not much to say about this one. I'll assume that you aren't the one the spark died for or you wouldn't be interested in rekindling the relationship. Even if the other person lost interest somewhere along the way, there are ways to get the relationship back on track – and hotter than ever! Keep reading to figure out what you can do.

Unhealthy Circumstances

Abusive, unhealthy relationships are usually the hardest to get out of. And even when you do get out of them, you find yourself wanting to or feeling obligated to go back. Be completely honest with yourself here: if you had an unhealthy relationship involving any kind of abuse, you don't need to be trying to win back that person. No matter how much you love them, you need to realize how lucky you are to be free from those circumstances and start now to move on.

If your relationship failure doesn't fall into any of these categories, make a list of things that went wrong or events that led to the end. Figuring out what went wrong is the first step. Once you know what went wrong you can start to move forward.

Unless you have a relationship that was unhealthy, continue reading to find out what you can do with what you learned in this chapter to win back your lost love.

Chapter 3: Take A Time Out And Focus On You

After a messy, painful breakup all you want to do is hide under the covers with Ben and Jerry – or maybe frequent the closest bar until you don't remember your own name. While these are both signs of grief over the relationship, and grief is a necessary part of healing, this should be a brief period. Take a week to truly be bummed out about the loss of the relationship and then pick yourself back up and start to move forward.

You can still be sad or upset and want your ex back, but the days of not being able to function should be minimal. Especially if you are trying to get your ex back. No one wants to come running back to someone who can't get out of their pajamas.

So, once you have allowed yourself a few days of sadness, get up off the couch (and take a shower!) and get ready to start winning back the heart of your ex.

First, evaluate yourself critically. Are there things about you that your ex complained about? I don't mean telling you you're fat and worthless. That is an ex not worth getting back. What I mean is were you always arguing over the same things? Did they often tell you to lighten up about something or have more fun?

Whatever those little comments about you were, consider them. If your ex had a valid point, then work on doing better at those things. However, if your ex was just being critical or saying things in anger that they didn't really mean, let it slide.

More than the changes your ex wanted to see consider the changes you want to see in yourself. Make a list of qualities that you find attractive in a mate. Attractive. Funny. Successful. Whatever they are, write them down.

Now, start today working on trying to be those things yourself. Look at television and movie characters that are successful or magnetic and try to pinpoint what they have. More likely than not, the things that attract you to others are also attractive to other people.

Confidence in yourself is one very important step toward being the person you want to be. It may be hard to be confident after being dumped, but once you start working on seeing yourself as the person you want to be confidence will follow.

Rather than moping around about all the things that went wrong in your relationship, concentrate on changing yourself for the better. That way, even if your attempt at rekindling the romance doesn't work, you will be ready for a healthy relationship with someone else.

You can't truly have a successful relationship unless you like who you are. The confidence and security that come from loving yourself will go a long way toward winning back your ex – and keeping them!

So take this time – before you start trying to win back your ex – to work on being the person you want to be. Go on a weekend trip alone. Not to grieve, but to recharge your batteries and plan your improvement. Take self-esteem classes. See a psychiatrist. Join a gym. Work toward that promotion at work. Whatever makes you feel more attractive, take time right now to do it. It will pay off big time in the end.

Focusing on yourself and regrouping will be a huge factor in making your relationship a success. Be sure to give yourself time to heal and get ready to be in a relationship again before trying to win back your lost love. There is nothing worse than winning back your ex only to make the same mistakes in the relationship all over again. Though waiting to start wooing back your ex is probably the last thing you want to do, it will help you have a successful relationship in the end.

Chapter 4: Re-Evaluate Your Ex

Now that you have had some time to evaluate what went wrong in the relationship and started working on yourself, it's time to think about your ex and if they are really worth winning back. There are many factors to attraction, and many even more complex factors to love. You need to be sure that the relationship you are trying to get back is worth it.

Also, you should consider that it is possible to love someone yet not be in a healthy relationship with them. Love doesn't fix everything. In fact, it can make a bad situation more complex. So, just because you love your ex doesn't mean that the relationship is worth salvaging.

Consider for a few minutes the things that you loved about your ex. Include physical characteristics that attracted you to them, personality traits, and anything else about that person that added to the way you felt about them.

Write these things down if it helps.

Now think about some of the things about the person that you didn't like. No relationship is perfect, and you will never find another human being that you like absolutely everything about. So it is perfectly okay to be in a relationship with someone that you find faults in. They can probably name a few of your faults too. Just because there are negative things about the person you love doesn't mean the relationship is doomed. However, there are some personality traits or characteristics that you may not be willing to spend the rest of your life dealing with.

Being honest when looking at your past relationship and the person you lost will help you evaluate clearly to decide if this is really someone that you want back in your life.

Also think about other people that you have been in relationships with or other relationships that you have observed. How do those relationships measure up to what you and your ex had? If affection is something that is important to you and your ex isn't affectionate, you have to consider how important that is. Or if they have an annoying habit that drives you crazy, that factors into whether you should try to get them back or not.

Think about:

Physical Appearance

You should always be at least moderately attracted to the person you are with. Think about how your ex measures up on the physical appearance scale. This attribute alone shouldn't make or break their attractiveness as a whole, but it will be a factor in determining if this is someone you want to be with. If you have to work hard to be attracted to them – if they have to be wearing your favorite blue shirt with the sun hitting their hair just right, you may want to consider looking elsewhere for someone that you are more physically compatible with. Let me say, that I'm not suggesting that you should only date models. What I am saying is that we are all attracted to different things about people and you need to be physically attracted to the person you are with. That doesn't mean that they have to be drop dead gorgeous.

Habits

Do they have habits that annoy you? Or do they do things that you particularly like? Make a list of both the pros and cons habit-wise about your ex to consider in how they measure up. There probably won't be any deal breakers on this list, but it is good to lay out all of the information about the person before you make a decision about whether they are worth spending weeks or months wooing back.

Job

Is their job a factor in the relationship? Do they work long hours? Travel a lot? Work in an environment full of the opposite sex? Have the potential to move around a lot? For most of us, work is an important part of who we are. Especially if your ex enjoys their work, you will want to consider work related factors in whether or not they are worth getting back. A relationship that didn't work the first time is going to be a thousand times harder to make work if it is long distance or you rarely see each other. Make sure that neither of your jobs is going to be a deciding factor in whether the relationship succeeds.

Past Issues

Whether they have past issues that predate you or whether those issues are concerning your failed relationship, you need to evaluate how those issues affect the way you see them as a whole. Anger management may be a concern or you may want to think about whether you can be with someone who is so emotionally dependent. Whatever issues they carry, make sure that you can live with them before you put yourself back into that situation.

Compatibility

Let's face it. Some of us are just more compatible than others. While it's possible to overcome compatibility issues, it makes life much easier if you share some of the same interests, live near each other, have the same goals, work the same general hours, and have other things in common. Make a list of the things that you have in common and the ways that you are complete opposites. Use this list to evaluate how your ex measures up.

Other

Every relationship and person is different, so look at any other areas where your ex might or might not measure up. Be sure to consider both the positive and the negative when evaluating your relationship to give you a true representation of what to expect.

After making this list, see how your ex measures up. If the traits on the "con" list are ones that you can live with, then you are well on your way to deciding to win them back. But if there are deal-breakers on that list, then you may want to reconsider.

Just because you are willing to put all of this time and effort into changing yourself does not mean that you ex will be willing to change for you. Ideally, you would be with someone who was willing to try to be everything that you want in a mate, but that is not always the case.

Do not expect the major things about your ex that you do not like to change. This will just set you up for even more failure. You have to do what you can to make yourself ready to be back in the relationship and then expect everything about the other person to be the same. They may or may not be willing to work on the relationship after you are back together. Therefore, you need to be prepared for the possibility that you will be in the same relationship you were in before except for the changes that you have made.

If you need to write down the pros and cons about your ex, go for it. Or you may be able to click off the list in your head. Either way, be sure to take a long hard look at the relationship you are trying to get back and make sure that it is really what you want.

We have all experienced the euphoria of the first few weeks of love. And while that is a wonderful thing to strive for, it is very hard to sustain. If that is all that you are looking for in getting back your ex, you would probably be better suited moving on and looking for someone else.

Relationships are hard work and you have to assume that you are the only one who will be doing the working – at least at first. For the relationship to work long term you both have to be committed to working together to make things better, but in the beginning you may be the only one working toward making things work. So, be sure that the ex you left behind is the one that you want back in your life.

Chapter 5: Get Rid Of Old Baggage

We all have a past. Not just the relationship that you just got out of, but everything that ever happened to you before that. All of those things affect the way you view the world and the way you treat relationships. But to make a new start with someone you have to leave behind some of the old problems.

If you need to seek professional help to deal with your past, please do. There is no shame in getting help to improve your life. Often, we hold onto things that happened to us in childhood or in previous relationships and they become a poison for our current relationship. If you feel like you have things in your past that you hold on to, do what you need to let them go.

Sometimes that may be easier said than done. Dealing with pain and other issues can take years. But start now working on putting your old baggage behind you. Even if your issues are not completely resolved as you try to win back your ex, the fact that you are trying to make things better should go a long way toward making your ex more secure in the new relationship. You and your ex will both be happier for it and it may just be the deciding factor in whether your relationship works or not.

Aside from the baggage, you had before meeting your ex, now that you have a failed relationship between you. There is plenty of baggage that you are carrying around concerning your ex. You have to deal with this baggage before trying to win back your lost love. You cannot go into a new relationship with a chip on your shoulder and expect the relationship to be happy and healthy.

It does not matter what the baggage is. It may be concerning the breakup. You may be holding onto an insult that was said in anger. You may be holding a grudge against that person for cheating on you. There are all kinds of things that happen in relationships, and they all create feelings of some sort – good or bad.

You have to put those bad feelings behind you before you can look to the future with your ex. If there are problems between you that are so big that you cannot put them behind you or that, you feel you need to go to couples counseling, then you have a decision to make. Often, whether or not you are willing to put that kind of effort into a failed relationship will depend on how much you had invested in the relationship.

If your ex is a spouse and you have children together, you will probably be willing to go further to repair the relationship than a couple who broke up after dating for six months. Only you can decide how much your relationship is worth to you.

You may need to seek counseling to work through the anger or resentment that you feel about your past relationship before trying to patch things up with your ex. Or you may be able to work through some of your issues on your own. Just identifying your baggage can be a huge leap in the right direction. You can write down your feelings about the relationship to discover some of your relationship specific issues.

Try using one or two word phrases to describe the way the relationship made you feel before it ended. Some of these may be negative, some may be positive. Whatever comes out, just write it down. You may be surprised at what you learn about your feelings.

Once you know, what you are holding onto you can work through letting it go yourself and put it on the list of things to talk to your ex about eventually if you two decide to make the relationship work. Getting your feelings out on paper, to a friend or to a therapist can release a lot of tension and frustration that you are holding onto.

Again, you have to plan to do all of the work yourself (at least at first). Any baggage that you have from hurt feelings to wounded pride have to be things you are willing to leave behind before you can have a successful relationship again.

CHAPTER 6: BEGGING NEVER WORKS OUT IN THE LONG RUN

The last time that begging and pestering successfully worked in your favor was probably with your loving parents, and of course, you had to be really young then. When you grew older, your parents became immune to your begging antics, not to mention that they had already mastered the art of saying 'no' to you.

Begging Will Get You Nowhere

The thought of begging never again crossed your mind until the day you broke up with your ex; you let go of your pride and went groveling hoping that she would have pity on you and take you back. Begging only creates problems for the both of you in the future and it is better to give up while you are still ahead and is considered to be the bane of all reconciliations.

Your Ex Will Think of You as a Charity Case

In layman's language, begging is defined as asking for something as a favor or a gift; a good hint as to why begging is one of the worst ways of getting your ex back. Why would you want your ex to do you the favor of taking you back; it makes you look like a pathetic charity case.

If you do succeed and your ex does take you back, they will only be doing so because they either feels sorry for you or because you made them feel guilty. A relationship based on such a shaky foundation is not bound to last and neither of you will appreciate the fact that you both feel obligated to be with each other; in the long run you will both feel like casualties of the unhealthy relationship.

You Will Always Question Your Partner's Motives for Taking You Back

After your ex gives in to your pestering, you will always ask yourself why they took you back whether they did it because they care for you and that they cannot picture their life without you or if they did it out of guilt and pity. A person's confidence can only take so much bruising from pondering on such damaging thoughts and feelings.

You will never respect or hold your ex in high regard again if you happen to suspect that they took you back out of sheer guilt and pity. It is only logical that you will no longer feel attracted to each other as before especially if you feel that your ex's feelings for you are not sincere.

You Both Feel Weak and Manipulated

Begging is a sign of weakness for all parties involved; first, you are weak for resorting to begging to win your ex back, secondly, your ex is also weak for accepting to take you back. A strong relationship is built by two equally strong people, never a pair of weaklings.

Once your relationship is built on a weak foundation, there is no chance that it will stand the test of time, and when it crumbles, it is difficult to piece it back together again. Making up a second time is usually a feat in itself, a third time is clearly a death sentence for your relationship.

The Foolproof Solution

Now that it has been established that pestering and begging will never be a lasting solution to getting and keeping your ex, you have to take another effective approach to fulfilling you goal. First, you should exude confidence by staying strong, showing your ex what they have been missing since the two of you broke up.

Show them that you are indeed worthy of a second chance and that you are mature enough for a new relationship with them. Give your ex some space and when they feel ready to start something new, take control by delivering on their needs and expectations.

Confidence and strength shows that you are proactive and that you have taken control of your destiny, not to mention that it makes you look more attractive. Begging is a sign of weakness and by doing the opposite, you remind your ex of the attributes that made them fall in love with you in the first place; your revitalized relationship will be more meaningful and more real than before.

CHAPTER 7: AVOID THESE 10 MISTAKES WHEN TRYING TO WIN BACK YOUR EX

There are so many ways that any relationship can go wrong. Some of them are immediately fatal, while others are just the moisture that gives the rust room to grow. Be on the lookout for both while nurturing your budding relationship with your ex. Aside from the specific changes that you have been working on in yourself, there are some general mistakes that a lot of people make in relationships.

To avoid going through the heartbreak of being rejected by your ex, keep these ten mistakes in mind and avoid them.

1. Stop Being Needy

Be an independent, fun person that your ex will want to be with. Do not constantly need to be with them or you will end up driving them away. Even if you have to fake your new found confidence, it will make the relationship much more successful. The easiest way to avoid being needy is to get a life outside of your relationship with your ex. Work. School. Friends. Whatever it may be, every part of your life that does not depend on your ex will make you even more attractive. When the time comes, you can introduce them into the other parts of your life, but be sure that your whole life is never dependent on another person. Not only will you be more attractive to them, but also if the relationship does not work out, you will have a life to get back to rather than moping around all over again.

2. Don't Expect Them to Change

You went through a lot to get to the point you are at – ready to woo back your ex. However, you need to assume that they have not gone through anything at all for your benefit. They are not the ones who have spent months trying to get back what you had. So do not expect them to be any different. If you succeed in wooing them back, in time, they will probably be open to listening to you and changing to make the relationship work. However, for the time being, they have no interest in changing for you. So expect to be the one doing all of the work and all of the sacrificing in the beginning of the new relationship.

3. Stop Bringing Up the Past

Yes, you have a past with this person. And there will come a time when discussing what went wrong will be a productive step in making the relationship successful again. But beginning with talking about what went wrong will not help you win back your lost love. No matter how much history you have or what broke you up, start by focusing on the good things. If you are the reason that the relationship ended, acknowledge the things you did wrong and apologize, but do not harp on the past. Start fresh and do not bring up old arguments or let resentment affect the way that you treat your ex. If you want to win them back, you have to treat the relationship as if it is starting new, not like it is starting again.

4. Don't Start Out By Putting Pressure on the Relationship

The words "where do you see this going" should not come out of your mouth for the first few months of the new relationship. Forget about trying to get back to where you were. Do not plan on spending the rest of your life with this person. Just enjoy the moment. Make it fun in the beginning - like all relationships should be. Forget about the future, just like you need to forget about the past. This is a time for enjoying each other and rediscovering all of the things that made you fall in love in the first place. Putting expectations on the relationship from the beginning will doom it quicker than anything else could.

5. Don't treat it Like the Same Relationship

The relationship that you and your ex ended, failed. So do not treat this new relationship like the same old thing. Start fresh. Realize that you have changed and that the relationship will be different as a result. Even if your ex is not quite ready to make changes to try and work things out, you should realize that this is a completely new relationship. Treating your ex like nothing has changed is the quickest way to end your new romance.

6. Don't Expect Too Much Too Soon

Your relationship did not end overnight. (Well, it may have ended that way, but there were many factors that did not just appear overnight.) So do not expect it to get back on track overnight. Take things one day at a time. Also, remember that your ex has lots of feelings about the previous relationship that they may be dealing with. They are probably hurting and may feel betrayed or abandoned. Depending on the circumstances of your failed relationship, your ex may need some time to get used to the idea of being back with you. Do not push them into a commitment too soon. Just enjoy getting to know each other again and give the relationship time to grow rather than expecting it to be fully developed immediately.

7. Don't Assume the Relationship is bound to fail

Just because the relationship failed, last time does not mean that, it will fail again. Going into the new relationship with this misconception will only doom the new relationship. You do not know what the outcome of the relationship will be so early on. Keep going day by and day and you will be able to tell eventually if the relationship is something you want to pursue further or if you want to end things. Either way, does not make assumptions about the relationship or your ex.

8. Stop Reverting Back to the Old You

You went through all of this trouble to make yourself a better, more attractive person. Do not let the relationship you used to have with your ex ruin the one you could have now. If you keep slipping back into your old ways, the relationship will start slipping back towards its failure. Remember that you are not the same person you were before the breakup and do not let yourself be pulled back into that role.

9. Don't Sabotage the Relationship

Knowing that the relationship failed before can give you the preconceived notion that it will fail again. Because of that, some people are inclined to sabotage the relationship by reverting back to their old selves or bringing up the past. Do not let prejudices about what happened before sabotage the new relationship that you are trying to start.

10. Don't Assume that Because They Loved You Before They Will Love You Again

The same old feelings that you both had for each other may come rushing back the instant you see each other again. Or it may take time to learn to trust and care about each other again. Either way, does not assume that you will feel the same way that you did about them before. Things have changed. You have changed. Even if the feelings you had for your ex before were good, they should be better now that you are trying to start a healthy relationship. Or you may find that things have fizzled and are not the way you expected. Do not try to establish a relationship based on what you think you should feel. Give the relationship time to develop so that you can see how you truly feel about your ex.

These ten mistakes are far from the only ones that you can make when trying to win back your ex. But avoiding these will go a long way towards getting your foot in the door again. Also, above everything, be honest. If you do something that, you are not proud of, apologize and promise to work harder not to make that mistake again. Very few relationship mistakes are fatal in and of themselves. Do not be too hard on yourself if you slip up every now and then. Continually work on yourself and the relationship to make it stronger and healthier.

Chapter 8: Tips To Get Your Ex To Fall For You Again

Just changing the way that you feel about yourself is not enough to make your ex fall in love with you all over again. You have to be the person that they want to be with. And good for you, they already showed that they were attracted to you by being with you the first time. So now all you have to do is rekindle that feeling again – and amp it up to make sure that it does not fail.

Start doing things with people other than your ex. Go to dinner with friends or out for drinks with co-workers. You may even consider dating someone else casually to get your self-confidence up. After you have a life of your own that is fun and fulfilling, start doing things to make your ex notice you.

Go to the places where they hang out. But make sure that you are not alone and that you look great! Do not ever let your ex know that you have come somewhere because of them. Take a friend with you to a place that your ex frequents, and if you see your ex act like they are not there. If your ex approaches you to find out what you are doing there, say something like "I'm really sorry. (Insert friend's name) wanted to come here for a drink. I hope it isn't awkward for you." Then proceed to ignore them for the rest of the time that you are there.

As hard as this will be, it works like a charm. The secret to getting your ex back is acting like you do not want them back. Don't you just hate reverse psychology?

But it can work in your favor this time.

More than anything else, having a life of your own that does not involve them will bring your ex back like nothing else will. And making them jealous will do the trick just as easily. The trick is to make sure that you never let them know that you are intentionally trying to make them jealous. Keep things light and conversational if you run into them. And never, I repeat NEVER, bring up the old relationship.

If your ex does not make the first move after seeing you out and about a few times, you can broach the subject mildly. For instance, if you run into them at a restaurant while eating dinner with friends, and they come over to speak to you, you can casually say "I was just telling them about the time we went to (insert place with funny memory). That was a great time." If that sparks a positive response, follow up by offhandedly mentioning that you are all going out for drinks after dinner if your ex would like to join you.

Do not let your first date back together be one-on-one unless your ex initiates the invitation. Keep things friendly and light and you will have them eating out of your hand.

To get your ex's attention (and keep it), try these tips:

Change Your Appearance

You may do something as simple as buying some new clothes or cutting your hair. Whatever makes you feel sexier, do it. Making improvements to your inner self should not be the end of the line. Just be sure that anything you change is for you - not your ex. Do not cut your hair just because they always complained about it being too long. Like everything else that you have done to make yourself more attractive do it for yourself – and whoever may want to be on the receiving end, not necessarily just your ex. When you make improvements to your appearance, you have more confidence and you automatically come across as sexier.

Show Off Your New Assets

Everything about yourself that you have been working so hard on put it on display. Whether you have been trying to get more confidence, have a life outside of work or lose ten pounds, show off what you have done. Do not do this by telling people what you have changed but by practicing your new skills. If the improvements you have been working on have taken hold, they will get noticed by your ex and everyone else.

Flirt with Them and Others

Do not use your new freedom only to woo back your ex. The more attention you get from the opposite sex, the more your ex will take notice. Forget about having eyes only for your ex. Flirt, go on dates and enjoy spending time with people other than your ex. This will boost your self-esteem and your wow factor with the ex. Talk about making them crazy!

Get a Life and Flaunt It

Make sure that your ex knows that you have a life that has nothing to do with them. Be busy when they call or make them wait to talk to you if they drop by to see you at your office. If you are, out with friends and run into your ex, say a brief hello if they come over and then immediately engross yourself in conversation. The point is to make sure that your ex thinks that your every thought does not revolve around them anymore (even if it does).

Once you have your ex's attention, get them to fall in love with you all over again by being yourself – the new you. Be honest, open and warm to them. Do not try to play hard to get once you already have their interest. Show them that you are genuine and open to a new try at the relationship. You want to win them back by showing them what they have been missing and then be yourself to make them fall for you all over again.

You are not going through all of this just to get them to fall for someone they think you are. Be honest and give the relationship a good starting point by showing them all the new parts of yourself that you have been working on. Try to find a balance between giving them enough to make them care about you again and leaving them wanting more. The best way to do this is not to hold back anything, but to make yourself less available (as far as spending time with them is concerned) than you were before.

Spend quality time with them rather than logging quantity hours onto the relationship.

Chapter 9: 10 Flirting Tips To Win Back Your Ex

If you want to your ex's undivided attention, then flirting is definitely key to the success of your new relationship.

But you can't just have at it, you need the right information to flirt the right way otherwise you could be sending all kinds of mixed messages, especially if you aren't aware of what you're doing.

Why Is Flirting So Important?

If you were to break down flirting to its scientific components, it's the universal non-verbal language of communication. It's how we interact and socialize with one another as human beings and how we meet potential mates.

Flirting expresses interest and is usually the pre-cursor to a relationship.

You're about to learn the top 10 flirting "do's" that can help you snag your ex partner's undivided attention all over again.

1. The Physical - How To Get Off On The Right Foot

Give yourself a running start by beginning with your physical appearance. The last thing you want to do is to meet your ex with custard stains on your good shirt or not having had a shower first. The time you take to groom yourself speaks volumes of you and shows that the other person was worth the effort.

Flirting is all about non-verbal communication and beauty is in the eye of the beholder so give yourself a good head start by ensuring your physical appearance is up to scratch.

Wear clothing that compliments your style and personality and body shape and wear something that will not only help you feel confident but is also comfortable. The last thing you want to worry about is regretting wearing a pair of pants or a top that may be a little too tight and end up making you feel self-conscious that you'll be too distracted by it to concentrate on your flirting.

2. Body Language

What you don't say is almost as important as what you do say. It's incredible how much we can interpret non-verbal cues as we do the verbal ones.

When it comes to your body language be aware of how you convey yourself, how you come across and how your ex portrays you.

For example folded arms and crossed legs send the sub conscious signal that you're closed off and have no interest engaging in conversation with anyone, let alone them.

Keep your arms unfolded. Make them an active participant in your conversation. For instance if you're not too sure what to do with your hands use them to express yourself as you speak but don't overdo it or you'll end up looking like a weather presenter.

If you're sitting at a bar, use your hands to hold the glass in front of you or to run your fingers over your necklace which subtly draws attention there without it seeming too obvious.

HOW TO GET YOUR EX BACK

When two people are engaged with each other they tend to mirror each other's body language, this can often be so under the radar you don't often notice it unless you pay attention. If your ex begins to mirror the way you sit, your body position and changes subconsciously when you do, then they're showing definite signs of interest.

3. Hold Eye Contact

This is an important one but if done incorrectly can seem a little creepy. You have to practice this one in the mirror to get the technique just right.

Holding eye contact is important to set you a part from every other person having a general conversation with your ex. Eye contact shows you're interested and engaged, yet on the flip side if done incorrectly can send the wrong message and make them feel uncomfortable.

Hold eye contact with them in 3 to 5 second bouts, then look away. Don't hold your stare for more than 10 seconds at a time or you'll come across as gawking or worse, daydreaming.

Another great way to break up the stare is to look at their face in a T-Shape.

Dart between left and right eyes when making eye contact and drop your gaze to their mouth, just for a moment. It clearly shows your interest and that you're scanning their face in detail and taking it all in, all without overdoing it. Your eyes are subconsciously telling them you're interested your attention is completely invested in them.

4. Smile

Don't forget to smile, a smile though a simple gesture can speak volumes non-verbally. Smiling not only makes your ex feel desirable but they feel acknowledged and that you're interested in what they have to say. So don't forget to smile, it doesn't have to be an ear to ear smile of the Hollywood variety just something subtle and not too over the top. Less is more, you want to win them back so you have to maintain a certain amount of mystery so that you can get to know each other all over again.

5. Look for Indicators of Interest

This is such a great way of gauging the interest of your ex without the fear of rejection of asking them outright if they still have feelings for you. It may not be the appropriate time to ask them to re-evaluate their feelings toward you and sometimes it's best to just play it safe, especially when you're just starting to get to know each other again. You want them to wonder where you've been all their lives and to do that you need to play it cool. So without going down the verbal route and asking at point blank range if they still have feelings for you, learn to de-code their body language and read the non-verbal signals for yourself.

Here Are A Few Signs Your Ex Still Holds A Candle For You:

- They mirror your body language, the way you sit and laugh at your jokes
- They seem attentive when you speak
- They smile and hold eye contact
- They make physical contact by brushing up against you or playfully touching you when joking or making a point
- Their body language is open and approachable

Here Are A Few Signs They May Feel Uncomfortable

- They seem distracted and completely disengaged with you, for example they may be looking everywhere else rather than at you
- They look at their watch and are keeping track of the time
- They get their wing-person to step in save them from you by acting as a diversion so your ex can slip away
- They turn their back on you while you're talking to them
- They walk away while you're talking to them
- They seem more interested in those around them

If these happen, don't pursue them, let them go. No amount of flirtation is going to get you anywhere at that point in time.

Maintain your dignity, smile and move on and without missing a beat, talk to another person without so much as flinching. Treat it as a "no big deal" moment. Your ex won't have the reaction they wanted. Don't look at your ex while you're talking to someone else. You don't want them to think that your tactic is only a ploy to make them jealous.

6. Compliment

Everybody likes a little flattery from time to time and compliments are no exception. Only give them if you mean it, there's no point in giving a fake compliment, be genuine or they'll see right through it. Compliment them if they look good, their hair, their dress, their smile, their confidence. If you've been a part from your ex for a while, compliment the changes that you see. No doubt they worked hard to make those changes happen so acknowledging this will make them feel validated.

Flatter, but make it genuine. If you try to flatter a woman with the "beautiful hair" comment and she knows full well it looks like a birds nest she'll be able to spot your compliment like a fake diamond. Women have incredible "spidey sense" when it comes to stuff like this so don't underestimate them for a second.

7. Keep Them Hooked

In other words, don't be a bore. Whatever made your ex snooze in your past relationship should be avoided at all costs in the new, improved version. Be exciting and engaging, don't waffle on about what you ate for dinner last night or that you've gained a few pounds since the break-up or are trying to re-salvage your life after the split. Maintain that element of mystery and show another side to yourself. Show them what they're missing and leave them wondering where this exciting person has been the entire time. Part of being captivating is how well you listen and how well you can recall details. If you just vaguely stare and nod that's not necessarily taking in and retaining information. But if you can work what your ex shared into the conversation it shows that you actually listened. Something that will leave a lasting impression on your ex.

8. Don't be too keen - Quit While you're ahead

If you hit it off again and things are going great, don't be overly keen to jump back into the relationship. Always leave them wanting more. That way you'll be on their mind and they'll anticipate seeing you again. Remember this is a new beginning, take your time and keep them interested by being just a little inaccessible without being too aloof. In other words, it's all about striking up the right balance meaning that you can't always make it to everything. You want to show them that you have a life outside of them yet they're still important enough to make time for.

9. Be Yourself

You should always be yourself, after all that's why your ex fell in love with you in the first place. Just be the best person you can be. You don't want to take on a completely different persona only for your ex to find that it's not the real you and feel deceived. Just be you.

10. Practice Makes Perfect

If you don't hit it out of the park the first time, that's okay. There could be several factors at play that are outside of your control. Perhaps your ex was distracted or maybe you were a little off your game, whatever the reason tomorrow is another day and another opportunity to dust off your flirting skills.

It's not always easy, being in a relationship for a while you tend to forget how to flirt but see this as an opportunity to sharpen your skills and to get back out there again with full confidence.

So there you have it, 10 easy to follow flirting tips that will help get you back in the driver's seat, keeping your ex spellbound and winning over their complete and undivided attention.

Chapter 10: First move

Who should make the first move? This is a complicated question, like so many that I am trying to answer in this book. But the main thing you should take into consideration isn't who makes the first move, but how the first move is made.

Of course, it is better if you can get your ex to make the first move, but if that is not working you can do it casually. As mentioned in the last chapter, make sure that you always keep things light and friendly. Never ask your ex out on a date as the first move.

If you are going to ask, your ex out you can do it one of two ways:

1. You can wait until you run into them somewhere and ask them to do something "spur of the moment" like have a drink with you and some friends. Or if you run into them somewhere like the movies (as long as they are not on a date) ask them to join you and your friends. There are lots of ways to turn a random meeting into a second chance for your relationship.

2. You can seek out your ex to ask them to do something with you. This one is tricky. Be sure that you are not calling to ask them on a date. If you and your friends are going to the game this weekend and you have an extra ticket you can offer it to your ex. If you can work it, out to "accidentally" run into them to mention your extra ticket that is the best way. If not, casually call them and act apologetic, like it was not your idea.

Either of these can work as long as you do not act desperate to have them do something with you again. If you are going to make the first move, be absolutely sure that you do not do it the first time that you see them after your breakup. Even though you probably want to get the ball rolling as soon as possible, time is your friend. Playing hard to get by having a life without your ex is the best way to make an impression, but it does not work overnight. You have to give it time to take effect.

When all you can think about is getting your ex back, patience probably is not your first choice, but it will be the best way to start out on the right foot. Making the first move is tricky and should be avoided when possible. Having your ex ask you out is your ultimate goal. But sometimes things just do not work out that way.

Give your ex plenty of opportunities to make the first move, again, without being desperate, before trying it yourself. Make yourself available to them (i.e.: Frequent some of the same places that they do, etc.) but do not throw yourself at them. It is hard after you have tried so hard to be the perfect person not to show them exactly how you have changed for them, but being aloof will get you further than being obvious.

Use mutual contacts to slyly get information about yourself to your ex. Do not say "Tell (insert ex's name) that I lost ten pounds." Say, "I've been working out at this great new gym and I already lost ten pounds!" This way the information gets back to your ex without the needy undertone of you being the one who told someone to tell them. Anything that you want your ex to know can be passed this way. Just do not be too obvious. Casually mentioning things about yourself and your life to mutual friends is the best way to get the "gossip" to your ex. No one can resist telling the latest information.

So, whether you make the first move or your ex does, make sure that you do not start off on the wrong foot by coming across as too needy. Playing hard to get and having a life of your own are the best first move you could possibly make.

Chapter 11: Getting Reacquainted With Each Other Again

This is the fun part. Getting to know each other the first time was part of why you want them back now, so take your time when reacquainting yourselves. Do things together that you have never done. If there is a place that your ex always wanted to go that you would never go with them, now is a good time to show them that you are open to their ideas.

Doing the same things that you, enjoyed doing when you were together before can be a safe comfort zone, but it can also lead to problems. The more of your past that you inject into the future the more problems you are asking for. Going somewhere that the two of you have history is better left for later when the relationship is more stable.

You may want to make a list of things about yourself that your ex does not know or a list of questions about your ex that you do not know the answers to. Do not bring this list out on your first date and start clicking things off. Just keep these things in mind to randomly bring up in conversation. The more new things you can introduce into your relationship, the more new and fresh it will seem.

Your ex will be pleasantly surprised by your new interest in them.

There is a fine line here, though. While exploring new experiences with your ex can bring you closer together, do not pretend to like something that you do not. The point is that you are trying things, not that you are pretending to be someone you are not. Your ex should appreciate the gesture of you trying the new activity even if you do not like it. Also, try to come up with ideas of things for the two of you to do together that is outside both of your comfort zones. This way one of you does not feel more confident than the other and you can use it as a bonding experience.

Here are some tips for getting reacquainted with your ex:

Include Friends

To help break the ice of a new/renewed relationship, include friends in your time together. Go out as a group to do things. Do not think that making a relationship work means that it always has to be just the two of you. Work on incorporating each other into your lives. If there is something that you and your friends always do together, invite your ex along. This can be a good way to get to know each other again without the pressure of a dating situation.

The Right Kind of Date

When you are trying to get to know someone – or in this case, getting reacquainted with them – choose the right kind of dates. You want to be able to talk and enjoy each other's company. Movies, plays, loud clubs and other places where it is hard or impossible to communicate effectively shouldn't be on the list of places that you visit regularly while trying to get to know each other again.

Get Active

While candlelight dinners are nice, there is something to be said for getting out and doing something active. Not only does is help put you both in a better mood by boosting endorphins, it helps break the ice and give you something to talk about other than your relationship. Learn to ice skate. Go bowling. Take a helicopter tour of a city. Whatever gets you out of the house and doing something together will help both of you feel more comfortable in the early days of rekindling the relationship. But be sure not to break the right kind of date rule too often. After all, there is only so much catching up you can do while skiing.

Short and Sweet

Keep things short and sweet in the first days of your new relationship. Long moonlit walks on the beach may need to be saved for later. Avoid getting too serious too fast which might scare away your ex before you have the chance to show them the new, improved you. Short dinner dates, drinks after work, a stroll through the park, anything that you can do in an hour or less is a good date for the first few times that you and your ex are alone together. The longer you spend together the more likely you are to fall back into your old habits – which is what we are trying to avoid. Keeping things simple in the beginning will give you a new foundation to build on.

Daytime Dates

Nighttime dates are associated with serious relationships and romance. So try out daytime activities together to ease your way back into the relationship. Whether you meet up for lunch or rollerblading, do it during the daylight hours. This will give you the opportunity to spend time together without feeling obligated to make things romantic. After you are getting comfortable with each other again and are ready for a more romantic setting, you can graduate back to nighttime dates.

Keep Them Wanting More

The more you give someone whether emotionally, physically or psychologically, the less they want. Be sure to always keep your ex wanting more. To do this, end dates or the time that you spend together before expected. That doesn't mean leaving them sitting at the dinner table to finish alone, but do not linger longer than necessary. Always have somewhere that you need to be – a work meeting, bed to get rest for an early morning, walk the dog – and be sure that your ex knows they are not invited to join you for this. Leaving them wanting more will put you in a great position in the relationship. Without playing too hard to get, keep the ball in your court by controlling the length of your dates. This will drive your ex crazy (in a good way).

Make sure that while getting to know your ex again and following these tips you are completely honest. Do not go overboard and tell them that you changed all these things about yourself for them, but tell them about some of the things that you have done to improve yourself. Tell them about your new gym membership or your ritual of going out for drinks with your friends every Tuesday night. Whatever you have been doing to get your ex's attention, now is the time to talk about it.

By keeping things simple and light you will set up groundwork for a good relationship. Do not try to start out where you left off. Treat this like a completely new relationship with a completely new person.

Chapter 12: When Should You Have "The Talk"

First, let's start by defining "the talk". More accurately it has the "let's talk about what went wrong last time and how we can both work together to fix it for this time". While you may be tempted to have this talk right up front and make sure that everything is in the open before you put yourself out there again, it is better left for later.

That is unless your ex also wants to try to make things work. The talk only helps when both people are ready to start working on the relationship. If you try to talk to your ex too soon it may result in pushing them away. The talk is a pretty serious step, signaling that things are taking a turn for serious again. After all, who wants to work on a relationship that is only going to last a couple of weeks?

Your situation is unique and if you feel like you need to have the talk immediately, than go for it. This may be the case for any number of reasons. Most often the talk should be your first move when: a) trying to repair a broken marriage or b) you are the person who broke things off and your ex is still interested in you. If these two circumstances do not apply to you, then save the talk for later in the relationship.

You will know that you are ready to have the talk when things start getting serious. You do not have to wait for a marriage proposal to do this, just wait long enough to be sure that the relationship is going to be worth salvaging. If you start to have the talk and your significant other is not interested, hold off a little longer. This is especially true if you are planning on introducing a lot of new things that your significant other needs to work on in the relationship.

When you do have the talk, make sure that it is productive. Avoid setting a time and place to talk. Try to let it come up naturally. Make sure that you both have time and are not rushed, but telling the other person that "we need to talk later" only puts undue pressure on an already stressful situation.

Rather than concentrating on the things that went wrong in the relationship, talk about what you need from that person to be happy in your current relationship. Leave the old relationship out of it as much as possible. The things you want to change may come from the past, but be sure not to use examples from your failed relationship unless absolutely necessary.

For example, if your ex was constantly doing things with their friends and leaving you feeling left out, during the talk, say something like: "I need to feel more included in your life. Can we do things together with your friends sometimes so that I can get to know them?"

Make your request sound like a positive thing, not a condescending remark.

Here are some tips to help you have a successful talk:

- Cover all the important/deal-breaker points
- Concentrate on positives – what you can do to improve the relationship instead of what didn't work before
- Make sure you have enough time and are both in the right frame of mind – like on the walk home from a romantic dinner

- Take cues from your significant other about whether it's time to have the talk
- Avoid being too intense, but don't back down on things that are important to you
- Don't use this as an opportunity to bring up every pet peeve you've ever had
- End on a positive note – tell them how happy you are that things are working out between you and that you want to be sure they continue to work out

Once you have the talk and your significant other is receptive to the idea of working on the relationship, it is time to start over with a fresh outlook on the relationship. You may choose to seek counseling as a couple at this point depending on the issues that you are trying to work through. But keep in mind that couples counseling will only be beneficial if you are both committed to it. If you need to seek counseling for something personal that you are working through, you may choose to have your significant other join you with the permission of your therapist. This can really help you bond and understand one another.

Outside of counseling, though make sure that you are not making the same mistakes that you made in the relationship before. And if you start seeing your significant other falling back into ruts that they agreed to work on, remind them gently.

When nurturing a new relationship, remember to pick your battles. Before starting a fight – or even a discussion – stop and think about what you are upset about. Is it really worth possibly losing this person over? By taking a few minutes to evaluate the situation objectively, you will take anger out of the game and make it much easier to resolve issues – if there is an issue to resolve at all. Sometimes your pet peeves are not things the other person needs to stop doing, but things that you need to learn to live with.

As often as possible relive the good times with your significant other. Whether they are good things from this round or the relationship before, be sure to remember the things that brought you close together. Look at pictures, watch home movies, visit special places or just reminisce together often. This will give you a stronger relationship by helping you focus on the positives.

Also, when starting over, establish new routines and habits for this relationship. Be creative and go out of your way to do sweet things for your significant other. Be thoughtful. If your loved one had a bad day, offer to take care of dinner and give a post-meal foot massage. If your significant other's car is out of gas, fill it up for them while they are in the shower to surprise them. There are a million different ways that you can establish good habits in this new relationship. Try to do something every day to show (not tell) the person you love how much you care about them. You should, of course, tell them how much you love them every chance you get too!

Starting a relationship out right is as important the second time as the first. If you truly want to have a meaningful, fulfilling relationship, do everything that you possibly can to make the relationship succeed. Your loved one will either reciprocate or reject what you are trying to do, which will be your signal that things are not working out.

Above anything else, remember how much fun it is to fall in love and relive that with the person that you love every day. Keeping the relationship fresh is as important as anything else when it comes to having a long-lasting love.

Chapter 13: Cherish And Develop Your Relationship

Growing a relationship is like growing anything else, it needs lots of special, daily attention. This may sound like a hard thing to do, but when you love someone it can be a real joy to make them happy. Remember that this whole book is about re-finding the joy in love. To do that you have to go into it with a good attitude.

So, when you have won the love of your life back and made sure that things are on the right track for a successful relationship, it is time to start working on the day to day grind of a relationship. Let's face it, every day is not going to be a good one. Whether you have an argument or one of you gets fired from work or your dog dies, life happens. And healthy relationships are about working through the hardships and always being there for each other. It is always easier to get through the hard days when you make an effort to have a successful relationship every day.

Check out these ideas for keeping things fresh and nurturing your relationship every day – not just on your anniversary or Valentine's Day.

Have Date Nights

Set aside a night once a week to spend time together. You do not even have to leave the house if you do not want to, but turn your phones off and send roommates or others who live with you out for the evening if you are staying in. This is especially important if you have children. You may find it easier to leave the house for date nights. It really is not about what you do as long as you spend time together. Have some specific rules about date night like it has to be just the two of you, you have to do something that promotes communication (not go to a movie) and the date has to last at least two hours. Whatever rules work for you, be sure that you make time for your relationship every week.

Be Unexpectedly Sweet

Saying or doing things that are sweet are wonderful ways to nurture your relationship. Every relationship is different, and what your significant other thinks is sweet may be unique to them. Whether they thrive on appreciation or affection, find out what makes them feel loved and do it often. Boost their ego and be sure to give them compliments whenever possible. The best gestures are the unexpected ones. Do not wait for them to ask you how they look, tell them they look great. Or better yet, pick a time when they feel like they look awful and tell them how stunning they are.

Give Hugs and Kisses

Never underestimate the power of physical contact in a relationship. Hugs and kisses are great ways to show affection. Be sure that you are not stingy with your hugs and kisses and do not expect sex just because you kissed your loved one passionately. Make sure that they know that it is okay to be spontaneous and loving without expecting more. Sometimes hugs and kisses should just be enough. Be sure to kiss your loved one every chance you get.

Show Affection

Showing affection is a wonderful way to nurture a relationship. Modestly being affectionate while in public or with others tells the person you are with that they are important enough for you to let the world know. Do not go overboard with the public displays of affection, but putting your arm around your significant other or kissing them on the cheek while in public goes a long way toward making them feel secure in the relationship.

Do Things Just for Them

Make sure that sometimes you do things together that are just for them. You will not have all the same interests, which is perfectly normal, but you can do things together even if you do not both enjoy them. If there is an activity that your loved one especially enjoys or a restaurant that they love, be sure to spend time with them selflessly doing things that are for them. Even if you do not enjoy the activity or the food, try to find joy in just being with the person you love and in giving them joy. Make it all about them.

Say Thank You

Showing appreciation for the person you love is especially important in helping them feel loved. It does not matter if it is a big thing or a little thing, be sure to tell them that you appreciate them every day. Try to be specific too. Do not just say, "I appreciate you". Say, "Thank you so much for washing the dishes since I cooked dinner". It is much easier to believe that you are sincere when you are specific. And try to mean what you say. Being sincere will go a long way toward making your significant other feel appreciated.

Say I Love You

Show your significant other that you love them every chance you get, but do not neglect to tell them that you love them too. Never leave a room or a house or end a phone conversation without saying I love you. Make it a habit to tell them that you love them. To make it more meaningful for both of you, you may want to come up with another way to say I love you that means something to both of you. The movie Ghost comes to mind. In the movie, Patrick Swayze's character does not tell his girlfriend "I love you too", he says "Ditto." This comes to have significant meaning for her in the movie. Making I love you special will help it mean more to both of you.

Go Back in Time

Okay, not literally. Although if you have a time machine, now would be a good time to back and avoid the heartache of the breakup you are trying to repair now. I digress. What I mean by go back in time is to act like you are a teenager again. Remember what it was like to be in high school and in love? You did crazy, stupid, childish things that mortify you just to think about. Do some of those things again. Write each other love notes – on paper, on the bathroom mirror, wherever. The more creative, the better. Also, while you are on your high-school kick, hold hands everywhere you go together and in the car on the way there! Go to a movie that neither one of you cares about seeing, sit in the back row and use the lights going down as your cue to start making out! The point is have fun, humble yourself and act like a kid again!

These tips will help you keep your relationship alive and make you remember why you wanted to save it in the first place. They will also make it easier to get through the hard days. Whatever life throws your way, having a strong relationship will make it easier to handle anything.

Chapter 14: Knowing When To Move On

This chapter is not going to be fun to hear, because sometimes relationships just cannot (or should not) be saved. But do not think of this as a completely negative thing. After all, you do not want to waste your life trying to make a relationship work that is doomed. While it may feel like your life is over now, you will be able to move past it eventually.

There are some surefire ways to tell that it is time to move on.

Your Ex Isn't Worth Getting Back

You know your ex is not worth getting back if you were in an unhealthy relationship. Abuse of any kind – physical, emotional, sexual – is a definite sign that your ex needs to stay your ex. While physical and sexual abuse are more easily defined, emotional abuse can be just as damaging. Always degrading you, insulting you or making you feel unimportant are just a few ways that emotional abusers prey on you. If you experienced any of these things in your relationship, then it is best left in the past. At this point, you need to do whatever you have to do to move on.

Your Ex Isn't Interested in Working Things Out

If you work on yourself, discover your issues and try everything you can think of to get your ex interested again, but they still are not having it, it may be a sign that you should move on. This may or may not include them being with someone else. Your situation is individual and you have to decide when you have tried hard enough to get your ex back. Do not do anything that you will regret later to try to rekindle interest. A lack of interest from your ex means that they are not open to trying the relationship. That might change in the future – or it might not. Either way, it is time to move on (at least for now).

Your Ex Isn't Willing to Work on the Relationship

When you succeed in winning your ex back and the two of you start playing with the idea of having a relationship again, you may consider your battle won. But at some point your ex is going to have to be open to the idea of changing at least some things about themselves to make the relationship work. You should not be the only one sacrificing to make things work. If you have the talk and your significant other either does not acknowledge that they need to change or refuses to try, you need to move on. As painful as it may be to end things after you have won them back, it will be even more painful to start a new relationship with them only to have it fail for the same old reasons.

You Do Everything and It Still Doesn't Work

Sometimes relationships just are not meant to be. If you both try to make things work and yet somehow they just do not, you should consider moving on. There are a million different reasons why a relationship between two willing people might not work out – distance, time, and religion – but the only one that matters is the one that applies to you. Ending things on good terms will help make the breakup easier. Though be careful not to try to be friends too soon after ending a relationship. This can just drag out the inevitable and make it harder in the long run.

So, how do you move on?

You give yourself time to grieve the relationship, first of all. Lay on the couch crying and eating Cheetos for a while (a short while), and give yourself permission to be sad that the relationship is over. But in this phase, be sure to accept that the relationship is over and not try to come up with ways to get your ex back. If you have tried everything, then accept that it is time to move on.

After you spend a week moping around in your pajamas, pick yourself up and do something for you. One of the best things you can do is go on a trip by yourself. Be sure that this time is not spent mourning what you lost, but recharging your batteries and connecting with yourself again. You do not have to go on a trip. Do something that reminds you of who you are and what you love. Treat yourself to something that you consider a big splurge – whether time, money or emotionally. Try to come up with something that is completely unrelated to the failed relationship. This is about you – not the relationship.

When you have given yourself a pick me up, come back to Earth and start living again. If you need to see a therapist, find one. If you need a new job, get one. If you want a new apartment, rent one. Whatever you need to start the next phase of your life, do it. And then start living again. Reconnect with old friends, go out after work with coworkers, spend time with your family, learn a new sport or start playing an instrument. Do things that enrich your life, not just fill it up with busyness. While all of these things will not take away the pain of loss or substitute for time when it comes to healing, they will all be important steps on the road to be yourself again. And remember, that there is someone out there made just for you who will make your ex look like a joke. When you find the true love of your life you will wonder how you could have ever thought that your ex was the one. And you will know that there is no amount of time that is too long to wait for that kind of love.

Chapter 15: Conclusion

Love is a fun, passionate, wonderful, scary, exciting experience. It is something that you should strive to feel as often as possible in your life. Getting your ex back should be about having a happy, healthy relationship, and not about needing them to feel whole.

So, work on yourself first. Make sure that you feel like a good, whole, worthy person before you try to make any relationship work. The more you bring into a relationship the more successful it will be. Being independent is a sure way to make your ex want you back and to keep them happy once they come back.

The tips in this book are designed to help you win back the love of your life in a healthy way. I want you to have a good relationship that will stand the test of time. Accomplishing that can be easier said than done, though. It takes time, hard work and commitment. If you are not willing to put in those things, then do not expect to get a wonderful relationship out. But let me assure you, every ounce of energy you put into making your relationship work will be absolutely worth it. In the introduction, I promised you that you would be know the following after reading this book:

- What caused the relationship to end
- If the relationship is really worth saving
- How to rekindle the romance
- Where to go after the "honeymoon" stage
- What to do if the relationship still won't work

Hopefully you have learned the answers to these questions and much more. My intent was to help you get started getting your ex back. Obviously I can't tell you every possible move that you should make when winning back your ex, but these tips should help you put to use the things that you know about yourself and your ex to light the spark again.

When you find the love of your life, you should do whatever you have to hold onto them. But if the time comes and the relationship is not working, you should also be able to be mature enough to let them go. Who knows, letting them go may be just what they need to decide they want to stay?

If you succeed in winning back your ex, never forget how lucky you are to have someone that loves you enough to work on a relationship with you. Sometimes repaired relationships can be much better than new ones – and they are definitely stronger. Use your breakup as a time for self-improvement and relationship evaluation. Then go out and win back the person you love.

There is no proven formula for getting back your ex, but if you use these tips adapted to your specific situation, you will see amazing results. Always take into account the person you are trying to win back. You know them as well as anyone, so use what you know to get them back. Be open and honest with them and you will have a good foundation for a new, strong relationship.

So, go make yourself into the person you always wanted to be and discover the joy of winning back a lost love! I wish you all the best.

Meet the Author

Jane Wymer is known among her friends as "The Matchmaker." It's not just that she has a sense of who will "fit" together, although she definitely does. It's that she's a student of people, and over the years she's gained a lot of wisdom in what makes people datable. She has a kind spirit and is often able to gently help people recognize areas that need some work.

The child of two therapists, Jane has been helping people solve conflict since she could talk. She gave pep talks to stuffed animals and advice to her elementary school teachers. During high school, she observed that while her classmates were obsessing about looks, the thing that really drew people to one another was confidence. She was the person who helped all her friends find—and keep—relationships, but didn't have one of her own. For the longest time she was great at unraveling anyone's love life, but in her own she was the classic over-thinker. When she finally met her husband, Mr. Surely-He-Isn't-Right, his mantra to her was, "Less thinking, more trusting." And it worked!

She and Mr. Right-After-All just celebrated ten years of marriage. They have two beautiful pups and happily meddle in the lives of all their single friends.

www.ingramcontent.com/pod-product-compliance
Ingram Content Group UK Ltd.
Pitfield, Milton Keynes, MK11 3LW, UK
UKHW022120230426
12048UKWH00010BA/624